THE WORLD OF NASCAR

TERRIFIC TRACKS: The Coolest Places to Race

TRADITION BOOKS®
A New Tradition in Children's Publishing™
MAPLE PLAIN, MINNESOTA

BY CURT CAVIN

Published by **Tradition Books**® and distributed to the
school and library market by **The Child's World**®
P.O. Box 326
Chanhassen, MN 55317-0326
800/599-READ
http://www.childsworld.com

Photo Credits
Cover: Corbis
AP/Wide World: 6, 10, 11, 16, 17, 19, 20
Corbis: 7, 8, 9
Courtesy Infineon Speedway: 22
Getty Images: 13, 14, 23, 25; Sports Gallery/Brian Cleary: 5, 28

An Editorial Directions book
Editorial Directions, Inc.: E. Russell Primm, Editorial Director; Katie Marsico and Elizabeth K.
Martin, Assistant Editors; Olivia Nellums, Editorial Assistant; Susan Hindman, Copy Editor;
Susan Ashley, Proofreader; Kevin Cunningham, Fact Checker; Tim Griffin/IndexServ, Indexer;
James Buckley Jr., Photo Researcher and Selector

The Design Lab: Kathy Petelinsek, Art Director and Designer; Kari Thornborough,
Page Production

Library of Congress Cataloging-in-Publication Data
Cavin, Curt.
  Terrific tracks : the coolest places to race / by Curt Cavin.
    p. cm. — (World of NASCAR)
Summary: Looks at the specifications and locations of four of the most famous racetracks
on the NASCAR circuit. Includes bibliographical references and index.
  ISBN 1-59187-033-X (library bound : alk. paper)
  1. Racetracks (Automobile racing)—United States—Juvenile literature. 2. Automobile
racing—United States—Juvenile literature. [1. Racetracks (Automobile racing) 2. Automobile
racing.] I. Title. II. Series.
  GV1033 .C39 2003
  796.72'06'8—dc21   2003008445

Note: Beginning with the 2004 season, the NASCAR
Winston Cup Series will be called the NASCAR Nextel
Cup Series.

TERRIFIC TRACKS

Table of Contents

4   **Introduction:** The Places to Race!

7   **Chapter One:** Daytona: The Granddaddy

12   **Chapter Two:** Charlotte: Night Racing

17   **Chapter Three:** Bristol: Slam-Bang Action!

23   **Chapter Four:** Talladega: Taking It to the Bank

29   The Tracks of NASCAR

30   Glossary

31   For More Information about NASCAR Racing

32   Index

I N T R O D U C T I O N

The Places to Race!

Every race fan has a favorite racetrack. In most cases, it is the track where they saw their first race or the place at which their favorite driver usually wins. In some cases, it is the track with the best view of the action or the place that has the tastiest concession stand food. Maybe it is the track that is closest to home or the one that offers the best chance to get an autograph.

In **NASCAR** Winston Cup racing, there are 23 different tracks in 19 different states that come in many shapes and sizes. They are located as far north as Loudon, New Hampshire, and as far west as the Los Angeles suburb of Fontana, California. There are two tracks in Florida, both close to the Atlantic Ocean (in Daytona Beach and Homestead), and one in the Arizona desert outside Phoenix. There is a track in the heart of the

Midwest (Indianapolis, Indiana) and a couple situated square in the mountains of Tennessee (Bristol) and Pennsylvania (Pocono).

The smallest track is in Martinsville, Virginia, a .526-mile (.8-kilometer) track shaped like a paper clip. The largest track is the 2.66-mile (4.28-km), high-**banked** monster in Talladega, Alabama. The track in Dover, Delaware, once held horse races.

There are two tracks in North Carolina (in Charlotte and Rockingham), and one in South Carolina (Darlington).

The best thing about all NASCAR tracks is how close the fans are to the action. At Darlington in South Carolina, fans are just feet away from the track.

Kansas has Kansas Speedway (in Kansas City), and Texas has Texas Motor Speedway (in Fort Worth). There is even a track—in Richmond, Virginia—that sits in the middle of a fairgrounds. There are tracks on the outskirts of Atlanta, Chicago, Detroit, and Las Vegas, too.

Today's NASCAR tracks are high-tech, fan-friendly, and filled every race day. They have come a long way since the short dirt tracks the first stock-car racers used. Here is a look at four of NASCAR's most famous and most fabulous tracks.

This overhead view of the Texas Motor Speedway shows how huge NASCAR tracks are.

C H A P T E R   O N E

Daytona: The Granddaddy

In the history of stock car racing, there has been only one NASCAR, but there have been two Daytona tracks—one on the beach, the other inland.

Exactly when drivers first challenged each other with fast cars on the beach isn't certain. What is certain is that five years after Bill France Sr. founded NASCAR in 1948, he began planning for a new track. It would be a 2.5-mile (4-km) asphalt track banked at 31 degrees.

In the beginning, the tracks were on the beach. Cars churned across hard-packed sand.

In 1959, it opened on former swampland as Daytona International Speedway, replacing a beach road course circuit.

The first Daytona 500 was thrilling. Its combination of
speed and banking produced a most memorable finish at 140
miles (225 km) per hour (20 miles [32 km] per hour faster
than the NASCAR record). Joe Weatherly, Lee Petty, and
Johnny Beauchamp crossed the finish line **three wide,**
though Weatherly was a lap behind. It took three days to
determine the winner. Beauchamp celebrated in **Victory
Lane** that day with an estimated 50,000 people watching. But

The Daytona International Speedway has been the
unofficial headquarters of NASCAR since it opened
in 1959.

days later, it was Petty who was named the winner.

Because the Daytona 500 is traditionally the first race of the NASCAR season, it carries extra interest for fans. Teams and drivers have had all winter to prepare their cars. The anticipation has helped make for some memorable shows.

Some of the most famous names in the sport have won the race over the years. Star winners include Richard Petty (Lee Petty's son), Junior Johnson, Tiny Lund, and Cale Yarborough. Greats from Indy-car racing have also won, including Mario Andretti (1967) and A. J. Foyt (1972). Benny Parsons, now a television announcer for NASCAR races, won in 1975. Richard Petty won seven times before he retired at the end of the 1992 season. Jeff Gordon won his first

Richard Petty was the most successful driver in the history of NASCAR and Daytona.

Daytona 500 in 1997, and Dale Earnhardt Sr. finally ended his drought in the race by winning in 1998. Sadly, Earnhardt died racing on his favorite track in 2001.

Perhaps the most important Daytona 500 was in 1979. People on the East Coast were still watching snow out their windows. Inside, they watched the first national live broadcast of an American race. And watch they did in record numbers. On the final lap, the cars of Yarborough and leader Donnie Allison hit each other, ricocheted across the track, hit the wall, and slid to the bottom. Richard Petty went around the wreck and held off Darrell Waltrip for the victory. A fuming Yarborough ignited a fistfight by screaming at Allison, whose brother, Bobby, joined in. It was captivating TV that the nation enjoyed. Daytona and NASCAR have never been the same.

Dale Earnhardt's victory at Daytona in 1998 capped one of the greatest careers in NASCAR history.

ANOTHER FAMOUS TRACK

Since the first Brickyard 400 in 1994, this race has become the second most important in Winston Cup behind the Daytona 500. It is held at the historic Indianapolis Motor Speedway.

Prior to 1994, the 2.5-mile (4-km) track was used only for fast open-wheel cars known as **Indy cars.** Some famous Indy 500 winners include A. J. Foyt, Al Unser, Rick Mears, Mario Andretti, and Johnny Rutherford. The Indy 500 has been held on Memorial Day weekend every year (except during World War II) since the track opened in 1911.

Indianapolis is a city that loves racing, and it shows by the fact that there are nearly 300,000 seats that always get used for the Indianapolis 500 and the Brickyard 400.

To be truthful, however, it is not the best track to watch a stock car race. The place is so big that you can't see the entire track. The lack of banking in the corners (only 9 degrees) means it is difficult for drivers to pass each other.

Indy cars are called "open-wheel" cars. Their wide tires are not covered by the car, as in NASCAR vehicles.

CHAPTER TWO

Charlotte: Night Racing

Charlotte Motor Speedway opened for racing in 1960. It sold naming rights recently to Lowe's Home Improvement Stores, so it is now called Lowe's Motor Speedway. Over the years, the track has provided many memorable and enjoyable moments. It's a neighborly race, too, as many teams and drivers live near the 1.5-mile (2.4-km) track.

Lowe's was the model for many tracks around the country. It has a D-shaped outline. It includes four turns and a fifth along the front **straightaway,** and has been copied several times. The tracks in Joliet, Illinois; Kansas City, Kansas; Fort Worth, Texas; and Sparta, Kentucky, are all almost exact copies. Of course, none of them but Lowe's can claim Winston Cup's longest race, the 600-miler (960 km) held on Memorial Day weekend.

Track president Humpy Wheeler has taken many bold steps with the track over the years. His biggest is challenging the Indy 500 whenever he can. That race is run on the same

You've got the best seat in the house for this racing action at the Lowe's Speedway.

14   Bright lights above and next to the racetrack make
      night racing at Lowe's possible—and exciting!

weekend as Lowe's biggest race. Wheeler's most important move came in 1992. That year, he installed a lighting system to stage the first **superspeedway** stock car race at night in 37 years. The first big one was an all-star race called The Winston.

The decision to race under the lights was made with the hope of adding excitement. That first race in 1992 (and those that followed) more than lived up to expectations. Three different drivers took their turns leading the final lap. Two of them would not make it back to the garage area in one piece. Dale Earnhardt Sr., leading Kyle Petty into the third turn, drove too deep into the corner and lost control of his car. Petty took the lead briefly but slowed to avoid Earnhardt's spinning car. Then Davey Allison slipped past Petty. Petty and Allison, both sons of NASCAR heroes, bumped several times down the front straightaway. At the end, Allison edged ahead to win before spinning and hitting the outside wall. Of course, the fans loved it.

UNDER THE LIGHTS

It might look as if NASCAR cars have headlights. You can see them when you look at the front of a car. But look closer: Those are just stickers made to look like lights. Even when racing at night, these cars don't use headlights. Teams battle to create the lightest, tightest cars they can. The extra weight and complication of lights is just one thing they don't want to bother with. Besides, at 200 miles (320 km) per hour, you don't want lights shining in your eyes. When racing at night, the cars depend on powerful overhead lights from the track, as at Lowe's.

Daytona is another track where lights mean night racing. Here's Jeff Gordon's pit crew working the late shift!

C H A P T E R   T H R E E

Bristol:
Slam-Bang Action!

Imagine attending a college football game in a stadium
packed with screaming fans. Add to that the excitement that
comes with watching a professional wrestling match. Put all
of this action in one place and at night amid a thousand camera
flashbulbs. Then factor in
the noise of screaming **V-8
engines** in fast Winston
Cup stock cars.

Welcome to Bristol
Motor Speedway and its
annual night race held in
late August. The Bristol

Fans at Bristol are so devoted, they even arrange to
be married on the track!

experience is arguably the most thrilling in American sports. That is why track officials keep adding more seats and why the waiting list for tickets continues to grow. In 2002, more than 160,000 attended the night race. It is easily one of the three most popular Winston Cup races on TV.

Most of Bristol's charm comes from its **intimacy**—that is, fans seem closer to the action here. But the rugged action on the track is compelling, too. Bristol is only .533 miles (.86-km) long. Its banking is a steep 36 degrees (the highest in NASCAR). On this tight course, drivers use their heavy stock cars to beat and bang on each other. Tempers usually flare in the tight quarters, too. Elliott Sadler is just one of many drivers who have thrown helmets at opponents who roughed them up.

"It is the toughest, nastiest little place you can go," says Rusty Wallace, who won his first Winston Cup race at Bristol in 1986. "But that's why we all love it so much."

Bristol's past is as interesting as its present. The land the track sits on used to be a dairy farm. The men who drew the

This picture shows just how steep the "bank" is at the Bristol track. It's like driving on the side of a hill.

Jeff Gordon roars under the checkered flag to win the
Sharpie's 500 at Bristol in 2002.

plans on brown paper bags initially wanted to model it after the 1.5-mile (2.4-km) track in Charlotte. Instead they decided they needed their own stamp on NASCAR racing. The result is a classic track.

The first race was held in 1961 before a crowd of 18,000. There were no lights around the track at the time. Atlanta's Jack Smith won the race, known as the Volunteer 500. Smith wasn't in the driver's seat when the race ended, however. He drove the first 290 of 500 laps. Then Johnny Allen took his place. The two drivers shared a first-place check of $3,225. By contrast, Jeff Gordon's victory in 2002 paid $245,543. The last-place finisher, Todd Bodine, received $76,634! The racing is still fast, but the money has certainly gotten bigger!

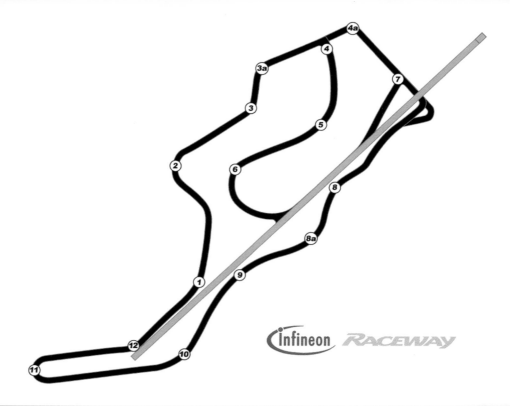

NOT JUST OVALS

All but two of the tracks NASCAR runs on are ovals (or nearly so). Two tracks, however, demand different driving skills. The twists and turns of the road cours-es mean drivers have to turn both left and right and use their brakes more often. The speeds are a bit slower, but the action is just as furious.

Infineon Raceway, once called Sears Point Raceway, has two road courses north of San Francisco. One is a 1.99-mile (3.2-km) road course. NASCAR drivers negotiate its 10 turns in a 218-mile (350-km) race. Ernie Ivan holds the track speed race record, set in 1992, at 81.412 miles (131.02 km) per hour.

The other road course is in upstate New York. Watkins Glen has 11 turns in its 2.45 miles (3.94 km). With longer straightaways than Infineon Speedway, the track allows slightly higher speeds. Mark Martin topped 100 miles (160 km) per hour in 1995.

This map shows the many twists and turns of the road course at the Infineon Speedway. The long gray section is used for drag racing only.

CHAPTER FOUR

Talladega: Taking
It to the Bank

W hen Daytona was
built in 1959, no
one had seen such
a large track (2.5 miles/4 km)
with such steep banking (31
degrees). At first, the drivers
thought it would be too
dangerous, and they didn't
want to run on it. Once on
the track, they experienced
a phenomenon known as
drafting. This lets a trailing

You couldn't put a piece of paper between these three
drafting cars, one after another. Drafting helps the
cars behind the lead car.

car go faster in the quiet air directly behind another car.

At Daytona, however, the trailing car felt like it wanted to lift off the ground in the swirling air. So imagine the concern drivers had in 1969 when officials decided to build a bigger, faster, and steeper track. They planned a 2.66-mile (4.28-km), 33-degree oval in the red clay soybean fields of eastern Alabama. They built Talladega Superspeedway, which is still the largest oval track in the United States. It remains the fastest and most competitive track, too.

If Daytona was a monster track like no one had ever seen, Talladega was even more so. And not everyone was thrilled. Some of the drivers decided to strike because they were worried about safety. The top qualifying speed was a stunning 199.466 miles (320 km) per hour, nearly 10 miles (16 km) per hour faster than the fastest speed at Daytona that year.

Because of the speed and size of Talladega, some of the most thrilling races in America have been staged there. As

Talladega's wide track allows for hard-charging, "three across" racing. Drivers and fans love the high speed in tight quarters.

of 2002, six of the ten most competitive races in NASCAR history were held there. The fastest qualifying lap in stock car history came at Talladega when Bill Elliott ran a lap of 212.809 miles (342.4 km) per hour in 1987. Mark Martin won the 500-mile (804.6-km) Talladega race in 1997 in a record-setting 2 hours, 39 minutes.

Shortly after Elliott's incredibly fast lap, NASCAR changed the way racing is conducted at Talladega and

Bill Elliott drove this car faster than any other NASCAR driver ever in 1987, setting a single-lap record.

Daytona. Officials called for the installation of what is known as a restrictor plate. This device reduces the amount of air flow in an engine, thereby cutting its **horsepower.** The result was twofold. Cars went slower, down to 184 miles (296 km) per hour in 2001. However, with constricted engines, cars were unable to break away from each other.

While drivers cheered the slower pace, they questioned the logic of pack racing. When cars are so close together, the margin of error is greatly reduced. That's why big accidents take place, they say. But that action is part of what makes Talladega so memorable.

Round and round they go, at tracks around the nation. Each track has its own fans, but every track boasts the best stock car racing in the world.

ON THE ROAD

People who work in NASCAR travel to different tracks—and different cities—each week during the season (February to November). Each city offers its own fun.

In New Hampshire, drivers load up on batches of fresh lobster. In Texas, a feast of prime rib is usually in order in Fort Worth's stockyard restaurant area.

In Indianapolis, there are Indy-car and drag-racing shops to visit. Hollywood, Disneyland, and Universal Studios tours are not far from Fontana's California Speedway.

A trip to Phoenix in early November usually includes a round of golf in wonderful winter weather. Drivers and their families plan time at the seashore when they arrive in Daytona Beach. This author's annual travel schedule has one highlight, however. At Talladega, driver Kevin Harvick's team owner, Richard Childress, serves up an interesting meal. He fries up fresh alligator meat just like chicken and puts on a real feast.

Fans, drivers, teams, and officials often travel between tracks in RVs, which they can park on the track's infield (bottom).

THE TRACKS OF NASCAR

Track	Location	Length Miles/Km
Atlanta Motor Speedway	Atlanta, Georgia	1.54/2.48
Bristol Motor Speedway	Bristol, Tennessee	0.53/0.86
California Speedway	Fontana, California	2.00/3.22
Chicagoland Speedway	Joliet, Illinois	1.50/2.41
Darlington Raceway	Darlington, South Carolina	1.36/2.19
Daytona International Speedway	Daytona Beach, Florida	2.50/4.02
Dover International Speedway	Dover, Delaware	1.00/1.60
Homestead-Miami Speedway	Homestead, Florida	1.50/2.41
Indianapolis Motor Speedway	Indianapolis, Indiana	2.50/4.02
Infineon Raceway	Sonoma, California	1.99/3.20
Kansas Speedway	Kansas City, Kansas	1.50/2.41
Las Vegas Motor Speedway	Las Vegas, Nevada	1.50/2.41
Lowe's Motor Speedway	Charlotte, North Carolina	1.50/2.41
Martinsville Speedway	Martinsville, Virginia	0.526/0.846
Michigan International Speedway	Brooklyn, Michigan	2.00/3.22
New Hampshire International Speedway	Loudon, New Hampsire	1.058/1.702
North Carolina Speedway	Rockingham, North Carolina	1.017/1.636
Phoenix International Raceway	Avondale, Arizona	1.00/1.60
Pocono Raceway	Long Pond, Pennsylvania	2.50/4.02
Richmond International Raceway	Richmond, Virginia	0.75/1.21
Talladega Superspeedway	Talladega, Alabama	2.66/4.28
Texas Motor Speedway	Fort Worth, Texas	1.50/2.41
Watkins Glen International	Watkins Glen, New York	2.45/3.94

GLOSSARY

banked—angled or tipped; used to describe how tracks are angled from the low end on the inside of the track to a higher end at the outside, near the stands

horsepower—a measurement of an engine's power

Indy cars—open-wheel racers with long, thin bodies that, unlike stock cars, are not modeled on everyday cars

intimacy—the state of being physically close to someone or something

NASCAR—the National Association for Stock Car Automobile Racing

straightaway—a long stretch of track without any curves

superspeedway—a banked, asphalt track longer than 1.5 miles (2.4 km)

three-wide—when three cars cross the finish line running very close together in parallel

V-8 engines—powerful engines used in Winston Cup cars, having eight cylinders arranged in the shape of a V

Victory Lane—a place on the track where the winner goes after a race to be greeted by fans and get his trophy

FOR MORE INFORMATION ABOUT NASCAR RACING

Books

Barber, Phil. *Stock Car's Greatest Race: The First and the Fastest.* Excelsior, Minn.: Tradition Books, 2002.

Cavin, Curt. *Race Day: The Fastest Show on Earth.* Excelsior, Minn.: Tradition Books, 2002.

Dutton, Monte. *Taking Stock: Life in NASCAR's Fast Lane.* Dulles, Va.: Brassey's Inc., 2002.

Fleischman, Bill, and Al Pearce. *The Unauthorized NASCAR Fan Guide.* Detroit: Visible Ink Press, 2002.

Web Sites

The Official Web Site of Daytona International Speedway
http://www.daytonausa.com
For a look inside everything that is the Daytona experience

The Official Web Site of NASCAR
http://www.nascar.com
For an in-depth look at each track on the NASCAR Winston Cup circuit as well as statistical and biographical information on all of the drivers

The Official Web Site of Talladega Superspeedway
http://www.talladegasuperspeedway.com
For a review of all things that take place at Talladega Superspeedway

INDEX

Allen, Johnny, 21
Allison, Bobby, 10
Allison, Davey, 15
Allison, Donnie, 10
Andretti, Mario, 9, 11

Beauchamp, Johnny, 8
Bodine, Todd, 21
Brickyard 400, 11
Bristol Motor Speedway,
    17–18, 21

Charlotte Motor
    Speedway. See Lowe's
    Motor Speedway.
Childress, Richard, 28

Daytona International
    Speedway, 7–10, 23–24

Earnhardt, Dale, Sr.,
    10, 15
Elliott, Bill, 26

Foyt, A. J., 9, 11
France, Bill, Sr., 7

Gordon, Jeff, 9–10, 21

Indianapolis 500, 11
Indianapolis Motor
    Speedway, 11
Infineon Raceway, 22
Ivan, Ernie, 22

Johnson, Junior, 9

Kansas Speedway, 6

Lowe's Motor Speedway,
    12–13, 15, 16
Lund, Tiny, 9

Martin, Mark, 22, 26
Mears, Rick, 11

Parsons, Benny, 9
Petty, Kyle, 15
Petty, Lee, 8, 9
Petty, Richard, 9, 10

restrictor plates, 27
Rutherford, Johnny, 11

Sadler, Elliott, 18
Sears Point Raceway.
    See Infineon Raceway.
Smith, Jack, 21
speed records, 8, 22, 26

Talladega Superspeed-·
    way, 24, 26, 27
Texas Motor Speedway,
    6

Unser, Al, 11

Volunteer 500, 21

Wallace, Rusty, 18
Waltrip, Darrell, 10
Watkins Glen, 22
Weatherly, Joe, 8
Wheeler, Humpy, 13, 15
winnings, 21
The Winston, 15
Winston Cup Series,
    4, 11, 12, 17, 18

Yarborough, Cale, 9, 10

ABOUT THE AUTHOR

Curt Cavin has been a sportswriter for the *Indianapolis Star* since 1987 and has written for *AutoWeek* magazine since 1997. He also does television commentary on racing for WTHR-13 in Indianapolis. His primary assignment is the Indy Racing League, but he also covers NASCAR's Winston Cup division. He also wrote *Under the Helmet: Inside the Mind of a Driver* and *Race Day: The Fastest Show on Earth.* He lives in Indiana with his wife, Becky, and two children, Katie and Quinn.